A Dangerous
Delusion

A Dangerous Delusion

WHY THE WEST IS WRONG ABOUT NUCLEAR IRAN

Peter Oborne & David Morrison

First published 2013 by Elliott and Thompson Limited
27 John Street, London WC1N 2BX
www.eandtbooks.com

ISBN: 978-1-908739-89-6

9 8 7 6 5 4 3 2 1

A CIP catalogue record for this book is available
from the British Library.

Printed and bound in the UK by TJ International Ltd, Padstow,Cornwall

Typeset by Marie Doherty

ACKNOWLEDGEMENTS

We have incurred many debts while writing this book. We have drawn heavily on Shashank Joshi's superbly researched volume *The Permanent Crisis: Iran's Nuclear Trajectory*, published in 2012. We are also indebted to Flynt and Hillary Mann Leverett's hugely important and indeed masterly book *Going to Tehran: Why the United States Must Come to Terms With the Islamic Republic of Iran*, published just as we went to press. We have inserted a number of their insights and stolen the JF Kennedy quotation about noxious myths from their pages. David Patrikarakos' very timely *Nuclear Iran: The Birth of an Atomic State*, also from 2012, has proved invaluable.

We would also like to thank a number of experts who have read these pages in advance and helped us form our judgments. Conflicts Forum in Beirut have been generous with their time, and we would like to thank Aisling Byrne and Alastair Crooke for reading the MS and making comments. We would also like to thank David Blair of *The Daily Telegraph*, Peter Jenkins, Ben Wallace MP and Shashank Joshi of RUSI, who have performed the same service. Our readers have vigorously disagreed with some of our judgments, but they have helped make this a much better book and saved us from error. All remaining errors are our own. We also thank Nicola Dawson for cheerful and efficient administrative assistance.

Authors' note

One point of terminology: we wish we could have found a better collective term to describe Iran's opponents than 'the west'. The current so-called 'P5 plus 1' negotiating team actually contains China, Russia, Germany, France, Britain, the EU's High Representative and the United States. But the alternative term 'international community' would be completely misleading, since the 120-nation Non-Aligned Movement takes a different view of the Iranian nuclear question from that of the US and its allies. It is also fair to state that nuclear policy towards Iran has been driven most of all by the United States and a handful of client states, of whom Britain and France are probably the most important.

'For the great enemy of the truth is very often not the lie – deliberate, contrived, and dishonest – but the myth – persistent, persuasive, and unrealistic. Too often we hold fast to the clichés of our forebears. We subject all facts to a prefabricated set of interpretations. We enjoy the comfort of opinion without the discomfort of thought.'

President John F Kennedy, Yale University Commencement Address, 11 June 1962

CHAPTER ONE

THE OFFER THE WEST TURNED DOWN

It was the early spring of 2005 and a team of British, French and German diplomats were arriving at the magnificent French foreign ministry at the Quai d'Orsay on the left bank of the Seine.

But the splendour of the Second Empire building did not match their mood. The negotiating team, which included high-flying John Sawers (now head of the British Secret Intelligence Service), had been fruitlessly searching for a solution to the Iranian nuclear stand-off for more than a year.

There seemed no solution. The European negotiators, under massive pressure from the United States, were adamant that Iran must give up its uranium-enrichment programme.

For the Iranians these demands seemed an intolerable humiliation for a sovereign state, and a classic manifestation of the western imperialism that had humiliated their ancient country for centuries.

The meeting had been under way for approximately 20 minutes, with no progress, when suddenly the face of the leader of the Iranian negotiating team, Javad Zarif, was wreathed in smiles.

'We have a proposal to show you,' he said. 'It is an entirely unofficial idea. It has not been discussed or approved by our masters in Tehran. But perhaps it might be something we can talk about.'

After these preliminary words, the Iranians delivered a PowerPoint presentation which amazed the European negotiating team. It was the basis of a deal and one, moreover, that offered genuine benefits for both sides, though both sides would have to make compromises as well.

Briefly, in the gilded nineteenth-century Parisian salon, a resolution of the nuclear stand-off between Iran and the west felt entirely possible.

The Iranians explained that they were not prepared to abandon their plans to develop centrifuge enrichment technology on Iranian soil. But in return for carrying on with their enrichment programme they proposed unprecedented measures to provide guarantees that they would never divert peaceful nuclear technology for military use.

They offered a solemn pledge that Iran would remain bound by the Treaty on the Non-Proliferation of Nuclear Weapons (NPT) – which obliges member states to subject their nuclear facilities to external inspection – for as long as it existed.

They said that Iran's religious leaders would repudiate nuclear weapons.

They put on the negotiating table a series of voluntary restrictions on the size and output of the enrichment programme.

And they offered inspectors from the International Atomic Energy Authority (IAEA) improved oversight of all nuclear activities in Iran.

The European diplomats allowed not a trace of emotion to show on their faces. But one official recalls thinking that 'what we had just heard was a most interesting offer. We realised that what we had just heard was a valid and coherent proposal that was in full conformity with relevant international treaty provisions.'

This diplomat adds today that 'trust was not an issue, because over the preceding 18 months we had got to know our Iranian counterparts and had acquired confidence in the Iranians' ability to honour their commitments.'

When the Iranians had finished their presentation, the Europeans asked for a break so that they could discuss the proposal among themselves. Once on their own they agreed that there was no way that the Iranian offer would be acceptable to their political masters in Europe. One witness puts the problem like this: 'There was not the faintest chance that President George W. Bush's Republican advisers and Israeli allies would allow him to look benignly on such a deal. On the contrary, if the Europeans were to defy American wishes, they would be letting themselves in for a transatlantic row to end all rows.'

So when they came back to the negotiating table one hour later they were studiously non-committal. They spoke highly of the Iranian offer, but asked for time so that their governments could consider it.

And when John Sawers took the Iranian offer back to London it was very quickly forgotten. According to Foreign Office sources, Tony Blair intervened to make sure that it went no further. Later Sawers explained to Seyed Hossein Mousavian, spokesman of the Iranian nuclear negotiation team, why the offer could not be taken up. 'Washington would never tolerate the operation of even one centrifuge in Iran,' he said.*

---

* Seyed Hossein Mousavian, *The Iranian Nuclear Crisis: A Memoir*, p173

So the peace proposal from the Iranian negotiators was killed stone dead even though the European negotiating team realised that it was both very well judged and in full conformity with international law. 'This was an extraordinary sleight of hand by the EU,' says one European diplomat close to the negotiations today.

The purpose of this short book is to dispel some of the myths and falsehoods which have distorted the view of Iran in America and Europe. We will show how Iran has often been ready to deal reasonably with the rest of the world over its nuclear ambitions. Iran was one of the original signatories to the NPT on 1 July 1968, and has for the most part obediently respected its provisions, and continues to do so today. As required by the NPT, it has not acquired nuclear weapons and its nuclear facilities are subject to IAEA inspection.

By contrast, the United States (and its client states in Europe, including Britain) has stood in the way of a settlement by refusing to accept Iran's right to uranium enrichment under the NPT. Moreover, the west has repeatedly made unjust demands, and at crucial moments showed bad faith at the negotiating table.

Western politicians have nevertheless issued a barrage of partial and misleading statements about the Iranian position. These statements have very rarely been exposed in the western media, which as a whole shows little interest in finding out the truth about Iran. More commonly, western newspapers and television channels have disseminated fabrications which have fuelled hatred and suspicion, and sowed misunderstanding. We will supply examples of this malevolent public discourse, and seek to put the record straight.

As a result of these misrepresentations, most people in the west can be forgiven for believing that Iran is an aggressive and malevolent power hell-bent on the acquisition of nuclear weapons. We concede that it is indeed possible that the Iranians are secretly pursuing a nuclear bomb. However, we can show that there is at present no convincing evidence for this belief. Any western politician or propagandist who claims otherwise (and there are plenty of them) is either ignorant of the facts, or lying.

Nor is that all. The United States knows with reasonable certainty that Iran has no nuclear weapons programme, let alone a nuclear bomb. This also seems to be the position of the IAEA, which is responsible for monitoring the activities of the signatories of the NPT.

So what is going on? Why all the anger, the endless barrage of rhetoric and the ruthless drive to isolate

Iran, which has led to the sanctions that are reportedly driving millions of Iranians to the brink of poverty and despair? We will suggest that a different agenda is at work, which has little or nothing to do with Iran's non-existent nuclear weapons. We will argue that the United States and its European clients are driven by a different compulsion: the humiliation and eventual destruction of Iran's Islamic regime.

The central purpose of this book, therefore, is to make the argument that confrontation with Iran is unnecessary. As the settlement proposed by the Iranians at the Quai d'Orsay suggests, Iran is prepared to deal with the west. It is the west that has repeatedly refused to accept the peace entreaties of the Iranians, that is refusing to deal with Iran on reasonable terms.

So we will make the urgent case that America and the west should return to the negotiating table to strike a deal with Iran. The alternative is yet more of the aggression and brinkmanship repeatedly shown by western negotiators: and ultimately the risk of an unnecessary and pointless war.

CHAPTER TWO

THE UNITED STATES AND IRAN: A TRAGIC HISTORY

The best way to understand the nuclear stand-off between Iran and the west is to look back at the historical record, and in particular the long series of hostilities and tragic misunderstandings that have marred relations between America and Iran. This is a tale which starts in the aftermath of World War II, when the United States took over from Britain the role of superpower in the Middle East.

Until this moment, the United States had been much more popular in Iran than either Britain or France. Many educated Iranians believed that the United States was on the side of freedom, and therefore saw the American War of Independence as a prototype for their own struggles against imperialism.

This attitude changed once and for all in August 1953 when the CIA joined with Britain's overseas intelligence service, MI6, in masterminding a coup d'état in Tehran. The victim was the Iranian Prime Minister, Mohammad Mossadeq, who had been installed by an overwhelming majority in the Iranian parliament (Majlis) two years earlier. 'Hundreds of millions of Asian people,' Mossadeq told the United Nations in 1951, 'after centuries of colonial exploitation, have now gained their independence and freedom.'*

Mossadeq's central grievance had been energy, and in particular the fact that the Anglo-Iranian Oil Company controlled Iran's oil. This company, antecedent of the modern BP, was considerably more Anglo than Iranian, and had been ever since Winston Churchill negotiated the purchase of its shares in 1914. In the words of Michael Axworthy, an historian of Iran, 'the British government garnered more profit from the Iranian oil industry than the Iranian government did (nearly double over the period 1932–1950).'†

---

* Quoted in Pankaj Mishra, 'Why Weren't They Grateful?', *London Review of Books*, 21 June 2012, pp 19–20. Review of Christopher de Bellaigue's highly praised *Patriot of Persia: Muhammad Mossadegh and a Very British Coup*

† Michael Axworthy, *Iran: Empire of the Mind*, p236

Once in power, Mossadeq nationalised oil, and British intelligence and the CIA set about extinguishing liberal democracy. After a period of devastating sanctions came the 1953 coup. The Shah (who had briefly fled the country) returned as puppet, but Iran's real rulers from this point on were the United States.

For the next quarter of a century, the USA had three fundamental objectives. First, it was determined to ensure a reliable and safe supply of energy. Second, it wanted unconditional support for the state of Israel (and until 1979 Iran was Israel's only ally in the region). Third, the United States, which claimed to celebrate democracy at home, wanted to squash freedom abroad.

For more than half a century the Americans have allied themselves with dictators and autocrats throughout the Middle East, and rarely has this suspicion of popular movements been more pronounced than in its dealings with Tehran.

Once the United States had reinstalled the Shah on his throne, it was determined to keep him there. The US supplied weapons to his armed forces, collaborated with his torturers and secret policemen, and helped him pursue his nuclear ambitions. In 1968 the Shah's Iran, as we have seen, became one of the founding signatories to the NPT, which remains the foundation text and legal basis for all nuclear discussions between Iran and the outside world. No analysis of Iran's nuclear ambitions can be conducted without an understanding of it, and we will deal with the subject fully in the next chapter.

So by 1979 Iran had acquired, with US complicity, the basis for a civil nuclear programme. Two German-built reactors at Bushehr on the Persian Gulf were expected to start generating electricity within a few years. Then came the revolution and its aftermath. Suddenly Iran was no longer one of the closest friends and allies of America, but one of its bitterest enemies.

One reason is that so many of the leaders of the new Iran had suffered persecution under the Shah, and resented deeply the diplomatic backing and material support provided to him by the west. To give just one example, Ayatollah Ali Khamenei, today the Supreme Leader of Iran, was tortured and sent into internal exile under the Shah's CIA-backed regime.

More significantly, the overthrow of the Shah, and the emergence of the charismatic religious leader Ruhollah Khomeini as Supreme Leader, challenged the world system that had been established by the United States after 1945. One of the greatest theologians of all time, Khomeini's teaching contained insights which went far deeper than anything the rationalists and materialists of the United States could imagine.

But the Iranian revolution terrified the Americans for another reason. The Shi'a religious tradition which Khomeini articulated with brilliance was a powerful threat to its system of rule by proxy. The Americans had formed a series of arrangements with client dictators across the Persian Gulf. These dictators tended to govern in the interest of an elite, normally using brutal methods. Examples of this could be found in neighbouring Iraq, Saudi Arabia and other Gulf States.

Suddenly there was a political philosophy, articulated with overpowering eloquence by Khomeini, which spoke directly to the hearts of the dictators' victims. Shi'a Islam has always been a powerful vehicle of expression for the underdog and the oppressed. No wonder that Khomeini's Iran was hated not just by the United States, but by Iraq's Saddam Hussein, the House of Saud and the other ruling families in the Gulf.

Nineteen months after the revolution Iraq invaded Iran. What followed was a calamity which bears comparison in the nature of its carnage to World War I. For the next eight years of this hideous war – characterised by trenches, human wave attacks and the use of poison gas – the west favoured Iraq.* It supplied Iraq with weapons, including the wherewithal to make chemical weapons, which Saddam used against Iranian troops and the Iranian people. It is noteworthy that Iran refused to use weapons of mass destruction in return.

When one ponders on the role of the west in the Iran–Iraq war, the US embassy crisis of 1979–81 (which occupies such a prominent place in the American

---

* An insider's account of US favouritism comes from Richard Clarke who worked in the State Department at the time, and later became President Clinton's antiterrorism chief. In his book *Against All Enemies*, Clarke described how the Iran–Iraq war quickly became a stalemate, with both sides suffering heavy casualties. His team was asked to 'draft options to prevent an Iranian victory or, as we entitled one paper, "Options for preventing Iraqi defeat". As the war dragged on, many of these were put into action. Clarke claimed that, although the Reagan administration wasn't allied to Iraq, it did not want Saddam Hussein to be defeated by an anti-American, as well as radical Islamist, Iranian regime.

'In 1982, the Reagan administration removed Iraq from the list of nations that sponsored terrorism. Iraq was thus able to apply for certain US government-backed export promotion loans. Then in 1983 a presidential envoy was sent to Baghdad as a sign of support for Saddam Hussein. A man who had been the Defense Secretary seven years earlier in a previous Republican administration was sent carrying a Presidential letter. The man was Donald Rumsfeld. He went to Baghdad not to overthrow Saddam Hussein, but to save him from probable defeat by the Iranian onslaught. Shortly after, I saw American intelligence data flow to Baghdad. When Iran was preparing an offensive in a sector, the Iraqis would know what US satellites saw and Saddam would counter with beefed up defenses.' (p41) consciousness), in which some 52 US diplomats were held hostage for 444 days, seems less than a pinprick.

It is not surprising that the Iranian leadership should have concluded that the United States was an implacable and ruthless opponent bent on the destruction of the regime, and prepared to use any means to do so. The support by Iran for organisations such as Hizbollah in the Lebanon and Hamas in Gaza, needs to be understood in this context.

The Americans love to present Iran as an aggressor, but this is at best a partial version of the truth. The Iranians have more than once sought to make peace with the US, most notably in the aftermath of the attack on the Twin Towers on 9/11. This event brought thousands of Iranians onto the streets in candlelit vigils. Iran's religious leaders condemned the attack. In the aftermath Iran offered the United States assistance in the war against Al Qaeda. It provided intelligence briefings and help in the war against the Taliban, and offered to rescue US pilots shot down over Iranian territory.* According to Barnett Rubin, now a senior adviser to the US special representative for Afghanistan and Pakistan, 'Iranian officials later

---

* David Patrikarakos, *Nuclear Iran: The Birth of an Atomic State*, p171

offered to work under US command to assist in building the Afghan National Army.'*

One eloquent witness to this courtship was Hillary
Mann, the US representative at a series of secret meetings
which took place at the UN in New York, beginning in
early 2001.† At one of these meetings her Iranian coun-
terpart offered 'unconditional talks' with the US. This
was very significant, because unconditional talks were
what the US had been demanding as a precondition to
any official diplomatic contact. The Bush administration
didn't take it up.‡ According to James Dobbins, the diplomat who led the US delegation at negotiations leading
to the 2001 Bonn Agreement on Afghanistan, 'in 2002
and again in 2003, Washington actually spurned offers
from Tehran to cooperate on Afghanistan and Iraq and
negotiate out other US/Iranian differences, including
over its nuclear programme.'§

---

* Barnett R Rubin and Sara Batmanglich, 'The US and Iran in Afghanistan: Policy
Gone Awry', MIT Center for International Studies, October 2008, p3, quoted in
Shashank Joshi, *The Permanent Crisis: Iran's Nuclear Trajectory*, RUSI, Whitehall
Paper 79, p19

† She eventually resigned from US government service over US policy on Iran,
having served from 2001 to 2003 on the US National Security Council as an
adviser on Iran to Condoleezza Rice.

‡ John H Richardson, 'The Secret History of the Impending War with Iran That
the White House Doesn't Want You to Know', *Esquire* magazine, 18 October
2007, http://www.esquire.com/features/iranbriefing1107

§ Joshi, *The Permanent Crisis*, p19

Iran's reward for its help after 9/11 was to be denounced in George W Bush's 2002 State of the Union address, linked to Iraq and North Korea with the famous line: 'States like these, and their terrorist allies, constitute an axis of evil, arming to threaten the peace of the world.'* This was an extraordinary remark from a US president, all the more so since Iran had been co-operating over Afghanistan.

Even so, Iran continued to engage with the United States. In May 2003, acting through the Swiss ambassador to Iran, Tim Guldimann, Iran made yet another offer of peace talks.† There is little doubt that, had the United States wanted it, a wide-ranging peace settlement with Iran could have been discussed during this period.

---

* http://georgewbush-whitehouse.archives.gov/news/releases/2002/01/20020129-11.html

† According to John Richardson in *Esquire* Magazine: 'This time [the ambassador had] met with Sa-deq Kharrazi, a well-connected Iranian who was the nephew of the foreign minister and son-in-law to the supreme leader. Amazingly, Kharrazi had presented the ambassador with a detailed proposal for peace in the Middle East, approved at the highest levels in Tehran. A two-page summary was attached. Scanning it, Guldimann was startled by one dramatic concession after another – "decisive action" against all terrorists in Iran, an end of support for Hamas and the Islamic Jihad, a promise to cease its nuclear program, and also an agreement to recognize Israel.' This was an extraordinary offer. But the White House ignored it. Its only response was to lodge a formal complaint with the Swiss government about their ambassador's meddling.

CHAPTER THREE

THE NON-PROLIFERATION TREATY

The NPT is the core text which provides the basis for all the arguments and disputes about Iran's nuclear ambitions. The negotiations between the west and Iran are conducted within the legal framework created by the Treaty.

Yet it is extremely poorly understood. This chapter explains in simple terms how it works, and the demands which it makes on signatories. At the heart of our argument is the assertion that if the United States and Europe were ready to adhere to the provisions of the NPT and accept that Iran has a right to uranium enrichment under the NPT, then a solution to the nuclear stand-off between Iran and the west could readily be found.

The NPT is a very strange, unbalanced and ultimately very unfair treaty, which places diametrically opposite obligations on states. It divided its signatories into two categories, those who possessed nuclear weapons prior to 1 January 1967 and those who didn't, and very different obligations were placed on states in each category.*

Those in the first category were permitted to sign the Treaty and keep their nuclear weapons. Five states – China, France, Russia, the UK and the US – qualified for this extraordinary privilege. Under Article VI, they undertook 'to pursue negotiations in good faith on effective measures relating … to nuclear disarmament', but no deadline is specified. In the 40 years since the NPT came into operation, none of these states has

---

* The NPT was opened for signature on 1 July 1968, and was signed on that date by 62 states including Iran. But only three 'nuclear-weapon' states – the US, the UK and the USSR – signed at that time. China and France did not sign until 1992. Today, 190 states are parties to the Treaty, five as 'nuclear-weapon' states and 185 as 'non-nuclear-weapon' states. The latter includes North Korea, which signed as a 'non-nuclear-weapon' state in 1985 but withdrew in 2003, having developed nuclear weapons contrary to Article II of the Treaty, though its withdrawal has not been formally accepted.

India, Israel and Pakistan are not parties to the Treaty. All of them have nuclear weapons but, having acquired them since 1 January 1967, they don't qualify as 'nuclear-weapon' states within the meaning of the Treaty. So, to join now, they would have to give up their nuclear weapons and join as 'non-nuclear-weapon' states. That is very unlikely to happen.

given up its nuclear weapons. The second category – 'non-nuclear-weapon' states – was forbidden under Article II of the Treaty to acquire nuclear weapons.

The 'nuclear-weapon' states were allowed to keep their nuclear weapons but did not have to accept IAEA monitoring of their nuclear activities. By contrast, the 'non-nuclear-weapon' states were forbidden to acquire nuclear weapons and were obliged to accept IAEA monitoring. Under Article III they were required to conclude a 'safeguards agreement' with the IAEA and to subject their nuclear facilities to IAEA inspection to ensure that nuclear material is not diverted for the production of weapons.

To sum up: 'nuclear-weapon' states were not expected to give up nuclear weapons, whereas 'non-nuclear-weapon' states were forbidden from acquiring any of these weapons. However, in return for surrendering their right to manufacture nuclear weapons, the 'non-nuclear-weapon' states were granted the right to develop nuclear technology for exclusively peaceful purposes. Article IV(1) of the Treaty makes this completely clear: 'Nothing in this Treaty shall be interpreted as affecting the inalienable right of all the Parties to the Treaty to develop research, production and use of nuclear energy for peaceful purposes without discrimination and in conformity with Articles I and II of this Treaty.'

So on the face of things the NPT gives all 'non-nuclear-weapon' states what it calls an 'inalienable right' to uranium enrichment on their own soil so long as they conform to Article II, that is, so long as enrichment is not for weapons manufacture. Argentina, Brazil, Germany, Japan and the Netherlands are all in the same position as Iran. They are all 'non-nuclear-weapon' state parties to the NPT. And all of them have uranium-enrichment facilities without being accused of breaching the NPT.

So far as we can discover, neither the United States nor the European Union has ever acknowledged in public (or even in private negotiations with Iran) that Iran has a clear right to uranium enrichment on its own soil for peaceful purposes.

This is despite the fact that the official view in the United States at the time it signed the Treaty was that the possession of uranium-enrichment facilities would not be in breach of Article II. On 10 July 1968, Arms Control and Disarmament Agency Director William Foster testified before the Senate Foreign Relations Committee about the NPT. In response to a question regarding the type of nuclear activities prohibited by

Article II of the Treaty, Foster supplied a statement containing the following:

> It may be useful to point out, for illustrative purposes, several activities which the United States would not consider per se to be violations of the prohibitions in Article II. Neither uranium enrichment nor the stockpiling of fissionable material in connection with a peaceful program would violate Article II so long as these activities were safeguarded under Article III. Also clearly permitted would be the development, under safeguards, of plutonium fuelled power reactors, including research on the properties of metallic plutonium, nor would Article II interfere with the development or use of fast breeder reactors under safeguards.*

On the basis of this interpretation, the United States signed the NPT. Yet today the United States refuses to acknowledge Iran's right under the NPT to uranium enrichment for peaceful purposes. This refusal

---

* Quoted in US Congress Research Service report, 'Iran's Nuclear Program: Tehran's Compliance with International Obligations', June 2012, p17

is completely understandable because, if it were to acknowledge Iran's right, the case for applying sanctions against Iran would disappear.

Nor is this the only example of United States contempt for the NPT. The United States and its allies are also in breach of their obligation to help their NPT fellow signatories develop nuclear energy. Article IV(1) of the NPT gives 'non-nuclear-weapon' states an 'inalienable right' to nuclear technology for peaceful purposes. What is more, Article IV(2) guarantees them assistance in exercising that right. In it, all parties to the NPT 'undertake to facilitate … the fullest possible exchange of equipment, materials and scientific and technological information for the peaceful uses of nuclear energy'. In other words, by signing the NPT, states in a position to do so promised to help others in acquiring nuclear technology for peaceful purposes. Offers of help have been made to Iran in recent years, but they have generally been conditional on Iran giving up its right to uranium enrichment on its own soil.

In February 2004, President Bush declared that states that do not already possess uranium-enrichment plants should not be allowed to acquire them.[*]

---

[*] http://georgewbush-whitehouse.archives.gov/news/releases/2004/02/20040211-4.html

If implemented, this proposal would significantly diminish the rights of 'non-nuclear-weapon' states under Article IV(1) of the NPT by restricting the nuclear technology they can acquire. In effect, the proposal amounts to amending the NPT for those states that haven't already acquired uranium-enrichment facilities, and without their consent.

There can be no doubt that the Bush administration was unalterably opposed to Iran having enrichment on its own soil. But did that change under the Obama administration? There's no sign of it in practice. It is true that on 1 March 2011, Secretary of State Clinton said that Iran 'would' have a right to uranium enrichment under the NPT 'sometime in the future, having responded to the international community's concerns.'* Clearly, the US remains determined to have the last say on whether Iran is allowed to exercise its 'right'.

---

* Evidence to the House of Representatives Foreign Affairs Committee, 1 March 2011, http://www.gpo.gov/fdsys/pkg/CHRG-112hhrg64869/pdf/CHRG-112hhrg64869.pdf

CHAPTER FOUR

NUCLEAR HYPOCRISY

We explained in Chapter Three how the United States and the EU are defying both the letter and the spirit of the NPT in their dealings with Iran. The purpose of this chapter is to show how the United States has looked with favour on allies which, unlike Iran, have adamantly refused to sign up to the international non-proliferation regime, in particular, on India and Israel, the latter probably being Iran's most dangerous enemy.

Israel refused to become a party to the NPT so that it could be free to develop nuclear weapons. Without this, the Middle East would be a nuclear-weapons-free zone today. Israel has a large number of nuclear warheads, perhaps as many as 400. And it has the ability to deliver them by aircraft, ballistic missile and submarine-launched cruise missile (using submarines supplied at knock-down prices by Germany).* It is in a position to wipe off the map every capital in the Middle East (and probably much further afield). It is guilty of nuclear proliferation on a grand scale. What is more, it is continually enhancing its nuclear weapons systems, most recently by acquiring submarine launch capability.

Israel's nuclear facilities, unlike Iran's, are almost entirely closed to the IAEA. They remain closed in spite of the UN Security Council passing resolution 487 in June 1981, calling 'upon Israel urgently to place its nuclear facilities under IAEA safeguards'. Israel has simply ignored this resolution and no sanctions have been applied by the Security Council to force it to comply.

Far from condemning Israel's introduction of nuclear weapons into the Middle East, the US never mentions the fact that Israel possesses nuclear weapons. It took a vow of silence on the issue more than 40 years ago: to be precise, on 26 September 1969, when President Nixon made a secret, unwritten agreement with Israeli

---

* Walter Pincus, 'Israel Has Sub-Based Atomic Arms Capability', *The Washington Post*, 15 June 2002; see also 'Israel's Deployment of Nuclear Missiles on Subs from Germany', *Spiegel Online*, 4 June 2012

Prime Minister Golda Meir in a one-to-one meeting in the Oval Office in the White House.[*]

Under this deal, the US agreed not to acknowledge publicly that Israel possessed nuclear weapons, while knowing full well that it did. In return, Israel undertook to maintain a low profile about its nuclear weapons: there was to be no acknowledgement of their existence, and no testing that would reveal their existence. That way, the US would not be forced to take a public position for or against Israel's possession of nuclear weapons.[†]

By contrast, Iran possesses no nuclear weapons. Yet, it is being subjected to ferocious economic sanctions imposed by the US (and not endorsed by the UN),

---

[*] Avner Cohen and William Burr, 'Israel Crosses the Threshold', *Bulletin of the Atomic Scientists* May/June 2006, p27

[†] For an instructive example of the selective blindness of the United States, consider President Obama's visit to Prague on 5 April 2009, when he announced 'America's commitment to seek the peace and security of a world without nuclear weapons'. At a press briefing on board Air Force One en route to Prague, Denis McDonough, a Deputy National Security Advisor, was holding forth about the President's plans for universal nuclear disarmament, when the following dialogue took place:

Q: Have you included Israel in the discussion?

Mr McDonough: Pardon me?

Q: Have you included Israel in the discussion?

Mr McDonough: Look, I think what you'll see tomorrow is a very comprehensive speech.

http://www.whitehouse.gov/the_press_office/Press-Gaggle-aboard-AF1-en-route-Prague-by-General-Jones-Denis-McDonough-and-Robert-Gibbs-4/4/2009/

sanctions that are bringing untold misery to many ordinary people in Iran.

One might be forgiven for thinking that the west is applying a double standard and that the proliferation of nuclear weapons is acceptable so long as it is confined to allies of America and the west. To be fair to the United States, that has been its publicly stated position. When John Bolton was Deputy Secretary for Arms Control in the State Department, responsible for the non-proliferation of nuclear (and other) weapons, he was asked about Israel's nuclear weapons capability and replied: 'The issue for the US is what poses a threat to the US.'* In other words, proliferation of nuclear weapons by allies is OK.

European states have not been as overt. But the basic policy is the same: Israel is allowed to have as many nuclear weapons as it likes, but Iran is not even allowed to have uranium enrichment on its own soil for civil nuclear purposes, 'not one centrifuge' as John Sawers put it in 2005 (see page 12).

---

* Richard Norton-Taylor, 'US Hawk Warns Iran Threat Must be Eliminated', *The Guardian*, 10 October 2003

Favouritism to India

Today, the US accords India, a crucial ally in South Asia, even more favourable treatment than Israel in nuclear matters.

India refused to join the NPT and secretly developed nuclear weapons. After its first nuclear test in 1974 revealed the existence of its weapons programme, international rules were put in place to prevent states like India, whose nuclear facilities were not all subject to IAEA inspection, from importing nuclear material and equipment. This made it difficult for these states to expand their civil nuclear programmes.

However, in 2005, the Bush administration negotiated a nuclear deal with India, which led to it, and it alone, being exempt from these rules. To put this into effect, the US pressurised the Nuclear Suppliers Group of states, the custodian of the rules, into making an exception for India. Most members of the group succumbed to US pressure only after several years of resistance: they saw how damaging to the nuclear non-proliferation cause such double standards could be. But the UK supported the US from the outset.

As a result, the ban on India importing nuclear material and equipment, which had been in operation for more than 30 years, has since been lifted. In other words, a ban which was put in place in 1974 because India had a nuclear weapons programme has now been lifted without India having to give up that programme or its existing nuclear arsenal. It pays to be an ally of the US.

In effect, India has now acquired the privileges of the five official NPT nuclear-weapon states without having to sign up to the NPT. These privileges have not yet been extended to any of the other three states that have nuclear weapons but are not parties to the NPT – Israel, North Korea and Pakistan – although Pakistan is striving to persuade the US that it, too, deserves such generous treatment.

To sum up: the US and its allies, which claim they want to see the Middle East (and the world) free from nuclear weapons, are applying ferocious economic sanctions, and threatening military action, against Iran, which hasn't got a single nuclear weapon. Meanwhile, they look kindly upon Israel and India, which have defied the world by refusing to sign up to the international non-proliferation regime.

CHAPTER FIVE

THE IRANIAN NUCLEAR PROGRAMME AND THE WEST

The Shah had grand ideas for a civil nuclear programme, and developed them with US support almost from the moment of the coup d'état which dislodged Mossadeq. The first steps came in 1957, when the Shah concluded an agreement with the US under the auspices of the American 'Atoms for Peace' programme. Under this agreement, the US supplied Iran with a 5 MW nuclear reactor and high-enriched (93%) uranium fuel. Known as the Tehran Research Reactor, it began operating in 1967 and is still used to produce isotopes for medical purposes.

In March 1974, again with US backing, the Shah announced plans to generate 23,000 MW of electricity by nuclear technology within 20 years, beginning with two reactors at Bushehr. In 1976, President Ford 'endorsed Iranian plans to build a massive nuclear energy industry' and signed a directive 'offering Tehran the chance to buy and operate a US-built reprocessing facility for extracting plutonium from nuclear reactor fuel', even though it provides a route to the production of fissile material for nuclear weapons.[*]

Iran's nuclear co-operation with France and Germany was also extensive.[†]

By the time of the Islamic Revolution in February 1979, work on the Bushehr plants was well on the way to completion. However, work stopped because of the unrest leading to the revolution. Later, the plant was badly damaged by Iraqi air attacks during the Iran-Iraq war.

After the Islamic Revolution, the US cancelled all its nuclear agreements with Iran.[‡] It also did its best

---

[*] Dafna Linzer, 'Past Arguments Don't Square With Current Iran Policy', *The Washington Post*, 27 March 2005, http://www.washingtonpost.com/wp-dyn/articles/A3983-2005Mar26.html

[†] For example, France made arrangements for Iran to buy a 10% share in the European uranium-enrichment entity, Eurodif, so that Iran could acquire its products, and an agreement was signed with the French company, Framatome, to build a nuclear power plant at Darkhovin. Co-operation with Germany began in 1975 and the following year contracts were entered into with the German firm, Kraftwerk Union, to build a nuclear power plant at Bushehr and install two 1,196 MWe nuclear reactors – and to supply fuel for these reactors for 30 years.

[‡] France, Germany and other western countries followed suit. Iran also cancelled some of its own accord.

to stop states that were willing to provide Iran with nuclear material and technology from doing so. This policy has continued until today.

In these circumstances, it was very difficult indeed for Iran to move its nuclear programme forward – the main reason why it has taken more than 20 years to complete the Bushehr project. After a series of false starts caused by US intervention, Iran turned to Russia to finish the job. Russia is contracted to provide fuel for the plant and to take back spent fuel, thereby eliminating the possibility of Iran reprocessing it to produce plutonium for nuclear weapons.

Obtaining fuel for the Tehran Research Reactor was also a problem after the US cancelled the contract to supply it. The reactor was out of commission for several years.*

In 1983, Iran asked the IAEA for help in the production of, inter alia, uranium hexafluoride, which is the

---

* In 1987, Argentina agreed to convert the reactor to use 20%-enriched fuel (instead of the original 93%) and to supply fuel, which was delivered in 1993. The US failed to stop this contract being honoured, though others with Argentina were terminated under US pressure. In 1991, China contracted to build an industrial-scale conversion facility, capable of producing uranium hexafluoride, at Isfahan. This contract was eventually cancelled as a result of US pressure, but Iran retained the design information and built the plant on its own. Construction of this facility began in the late 1990s and it was declared to the IAEA in 2000.

feedstock for a centrifuge enrichment plant. While the IAEA's technical co-operation department sanctioned some assistance, plans to do so were dropped when the US objected. The IAEA is obliged by its statute to assist NPT signatory states with their civil nuclear programmes, but the US prevented it from doing so.

Enter AQ Khan

So the history of Iran's nuclear programme can be divided into two periods. During the first period, which ended abruptly with the Islamic Revolution, there was little difficulty obtaining help from the United States and western countries. During the second stage, as we have seen, America and other western countries did their best to prevent Iran from obtaining nuclear technology from abroad.

So, if Iran was to advance its peaceful nuclear programme, it had no option but to rely on its own devices as far as possible, and if necessary to seek to obtain anything useful that was available on the black market. In the mid 1980s (after its 1983 approach to the IAEA) Iran decided to turn to the black market for help in developing its own uranium-enrichment capability in the form of a gas centrifuge programme. It turned in particular to the controversial nuclear scientist

AQ Khan, father of the Pakistani bomb and regarded as the world's most important nuclear proliferator.

The AQ Khan network provided the design information for uranium-enrichment facilities and related equipment which, more than a decade later, enabled Iran to build an enrichment plant at Natanz.

Bear in mind that, in Article IV(2) of the NPT, states promised to share nuclear technology for peaceful purposes. To be precise, they undertook to 'facilitate … the fullest possible exchange of equipment, materials and scientific and technological information for the peaceful uses of nuclear energy'. Clearly the west, led by the US, has not fulfilled that undertaking in respect of Iran since 1979. This amounts to a serious – and continuing – breach of the NPT.

No doubt, they would argue in their defence that Article IV(2) only applies to the 'peaceful uses of nuclear energy'. But, the cessation of co-operation was not triggered by a sudden discovery that Iran was engaged in uses of nuclear energy that were not peaceful. It was triggered by a change of regime to one that wasn't to the west's taste and by a consequent assumption that such a regime could not be relied upon to respect its NPT obligations. It was done for political reasons.

It is entirely understandable that many observers at the time and since have been disturbed by the connection between Iran and AQ Khan, given his reputation. However, it is by no means clear that Iran breached its obligations under the NPT, or any other international treaty, in its relations with AQ Khan or in building the enrichment plant at Natanz. Nor was the fact Iran had obtained information covertly from the AQ Khan network of itself evidence that its nuclear programme had a military aspect. Its behaviour is explicable as a rational response to the inability to purchase materials and equipment for its nuclear programme openly from abroad because of sanctions by the west enforced by the US.

US intelligence is convinced that Iran had an active nuclear weapons programme during this period. But it is by no means an infallible judge – for instance, it was wrong over Saddam's WMD during the same period. In November 2007, it expressed the opinion that Iran halted its weapons programme in the autumn of 2003 and hadn't restarted it since.*

---

* US National Intelligence Estimate, 'Iran: Nuclear Intentions and Capabilities', November 2007

In its report of November 2011, the IAEA said there were 'possible military dimensions' to Iran's nuclear programme up to 2003, and perhaps afterwards.

In their recently published book, Flynt and Hillary Mann Leverett claim that over the past 20 years, no western intelligence agency 'has come remotely close to producing hard evidence that Iran is trying to fabricate weapons.'*

Nevertheless, it was the Natanz plant which precipitated the nuclear stand-off through which the world is living today.

---

* Flynt Leverett and Hillary Mann Leverett, *Going to Tehran: Why the United States Must Come to Terms With the Islamic Republic of Iran*: 'American, Israeli and other Western intelligence services have claimed since the early 1990s that Iran is three to five years away from acquiring nuclear weapons; at times, Israel has offered more alarmist figures. But twenty years into this resetting forecast, no Western agency has come remotely close to producing hard evidence that Iran is trying to fabricate weapons. In Russia, which has its own extensive intelligence and nuclear weapons communities and close contacts with the Iranian nuclear program, high-level officials say publicly that Iran is not seeking to build nuclear weapons. ... Mohamed ElBaradei, who served as director general of the IAEA from 1997 to 2009 ... has said on multiple occasions that there is no evidence that Iran is trying to build nuclear weapons.' (pp81–2)

CHAPTER SIX

HOW THE WEST SCUPPERED A DEAL

Today's nuclear stand-off dates back to 14 August 2002, when the Mujahedin-e-Khalq, the militant Iranian opposition group dedicated to the downfall of the Islamic regime in Tehran, revealed the existence of the uranium-enrichment facility at Natanz. This revelation was seized on as the excuse for widespread accusations, most vocally from the US and Israel, that Iran was developing nuclear weapons.

It is true that, in August 2002, Iran had not declared this plant to the IAEA. But Iran was under no obligation to do so. Under the safeguards agreement in operation between the IAEA and Iran at the time, Iran was merely required to inform the IAEA about additional nuclear facilities 180 days before introducing nuclear material into them. This was confirmed by the IAEA Director General, Dr Mohamed ElBaradei,* in his report to the IAEA Board of Governors on 6 June 2003.†

---

* Then the Director General of the IAEA. In July 2009 Dr ElBaradei was replaced by Yukiya Amano, formerly Japan's ambassador to the IAEA. WikiLeaks cables from the 'US mission to the IAEA' to the US State Department demonstrate the closeness of Amano's relationship with the US. He had been elected by the narrowest of margins over the South African ambassador to the IAEA, Abdul Minty, thanks largely to US support. At a meeting on 16 September 2009 with the US NPT Special Representative Susan Burk, he acknowledged his debt to the US in this regard, saying to her 'if you are determined, the US can do anything!' (See cable dated 16 October 2009 at http://www.guardian.co.uk/world/us-embassy-cables-documents/230076)

The US looked forward with enthusiasm to Amano replacing ElBaradei. In a cable dated 7 July 2009 (see http://www.guardian.co.uk/world/us-embassy-cables-documents/215499), the American Chargé d'Affaires, Geoffrey Pyatt, wrote: 'The IAEA transition that will come as DG ElBaradei's term ends November 30 provides a once-a-decade opportunity to overcome bureaucratic inertia, modernize Agency operations, and position the new director general for strong leadership from the DG's office.' In the October cable cited above, he was described as 'DG of all states, but in agreement with us'. According to the same cable: 'Amano reminded [the] ambassador on several occasions that he [Amano] would need to make concessions to the G-77 [the developing countries group], which correctly required him to be fair-minded and independent, but that he was solidly in the US court on every key strategic decision, from high-level personnel appointments to the handling of Iran's alleged nuclear weapons program.' The October cable ended by saying that 'his willingness to speak candidly with US interlocutors on his strategy and various balancing acts bodes well for our future relationship'.

† Paragraph 15 of ElBaradei's report. The Mujahedin-e-Khalq also revealed the existence of a heavy-water generation plant at Arak. There was no requirement to declare this to the IAEA since 'heavy-water production facilities are not

Critics say that Iran would have been better off declaring Natanz from the beginning, because not doing so made it look secretive and suspicious, and led to such dramatic consequences. Perhaps so, but the country was acting within its rights.

Despite the fact that Iran had not breached its safeguards agreement, Iran's nuclear activities at once came under intense scrutiny by the IAEA, scrutiny which hasn't ceased a decade later. It should be emphasised that despite this intense scrutiny, the IAEA has never uncovered in Iran any attempted diversion of nuclear material for military use. This fundamental fact is almost entirely absent from mainstream media reports on the Iranian nuclear programme.

However, the IAEA did discover that in a number of instances Iran had failed to meet its reporting obligations under its safeguards agreement, for example, a 'failure to declare the import of natural uranium in 1991'.* The quantities of nuclear material involved

---

nuclear facilities under comprehensive NPT safeguards agreements, and are thus not required to be declared to the Agency thereunder' (ibid, paragraph 5). Subsequently, Iran has begun to build a heavy-water research reactor at Arak, which is under IAEA safeguards.

* Paragraph 32 of ElBaradei's report

were small* and, according to Dr ElBaradei, there was 'no evidence that the previously undeclared nuclear material and activities referred to above were related to a nuclear weapons programme'.† There has never been any suggestion that these reporting failures had a military aspect.

After the revelation of the Natanz plant, the United States had only one objective in mind – to use the revelation to persuade the IAEA Board to report Iran to the Security Council, so that sanctions could be applied to force it to cease its nuclear programme altogether, or at the very least cease uranium enrichment.

At first, European states (aka the EU3 of Britain, France and Germany) tried to hold the ring between Iran and the United States. In October 2003 their foreign ministers visited Tehran, and an understanding was reached. Iran agreed to upgrade its

---

* Commenting on these failures, Dr ElBaradei wrote: 'Although the quantities of nuclear material involved have not been large, and the material would need further processing before being suitable for use as the fissile material component of a nuclear explosive device, the number of failures by Iran to report the material, facilities and activities in question in a timely manner as it is obliged to do pursuant to its Safeguards Agreement is a matter of concern. While these failures are in the process of being rectified by Iran, the process of verifying the correctness and completeness of the Iranian declarations is still ongoing.' (Report to IAEA Board, 6 June 2003, paragraph 33)

† Report to IAEA Board on 10 November 2003, paragraph 52

safeguards agreement with the IAEA and suspend uranium enrichment while further negotiations were taking place.

This agreement enabled the EU3 to successfully oppose an attempt led by the US to have Iran indicted for 'non-compliance' with its safeguards agreement and reported to the Security Council. This was a most unusual moment: the UK opposed the US in an international forum.

These negotiations with the EU3 led to the Paris Agreement, signed on 15 November 2004 in the Quai d'Orsay in Paris.* The Paris Agreement set out a road map for the negotiation of comprehensive long-term arrangements on nuclear, technological and economic co-operation and on security issues.

The EU3 appeared to accept the continuation of Iran's nuclear programme, including uranium enrichment, once 'objective guarantees' were put in place to give confidence to the outside world that the programme was for exclusively peaceful purposes. The agreement stated that the EU3 'recognise Iran's rights under the NPT' and that the final arrangements 'will provide objective guarantees that Iran's nuclear programme

---

* http://www.iaea.org/Publications/Documents/Infcircs/2004/infcirc637.pdf

is exclusively for peaceful purposes'. These 'objective guarantees' were to be in addition to Iran's obligations under its safeguards agreement with the IAEA, which is required under the NPT.

In return Iran agreed to suspend its nuclear activities 'on a voluntary basis' as a confidence-building measure and to sustain the suspension 'while negotiations proceed'. For its part, the EU agreed to oppose the reference of Iran's nuclear case to the Security Council.

The Paris Agreement was the high point of negotiations. A comprehensive settlement seemed to be within reach. It looked as if the IAEA would soon give Iran's nuclear activities a clean bill of health. As Dr ElBaradei wrote later:

> For several months, expectations that the negotiations would lead to an overall diplomatic solution were high. Iran's co-operation with the IAEA stayed strong; there were only a few remaining inspection issues. At the March 2005 Board meeting, Iran's nuclear program was not on the agenda for the first time in almost two years ...*

---

* Mohamed ElBaradei, *The Age of Deception*, p143

However, within a few months it became clear that the EU3 had been acting in bad faith, and were in reality not in the least bit interested in devising appropriate 'objective guarantees'.* Their objective was to force Iran to abandon a very important element of its programme – the production of reactor fuel by uranium enrichment.

There is no reason to doubt that the United States was behind this stance. The following year Seymour Hersh in *The New Yorker* magazine revealed the extent to which the US was dictating events from behind the scenes. He claimed that in early 2006 US Under-Secretary of State for Arms Control, Robert Joseph, delivered the following blunt message to the IAEA Director General: 'We cannot have a single centrifuge spinning in Iran. Iran is a direct threat to the national security of the United States and our allies,

---

* An account of the negotiations after the Paris Agreement, including Iran's proposals, can be found in Chapter 4 of *The Iranian Nuclear Crisis* by Seyed Hossein Mousavian. In November 2005, after the negotiations failed, Iran set out its case for its nuclear programme in a 6,000-word advertisement in *The New York Times*, entitled 'An Unnecessary Crisis: Setting the Record Straight about Iran's Nuclear Program' (see http://www.payvand.com/news/05/nov/1211.html). In addition, the Arms Control Association has compiled a very useful 'History of Official Proposals on the Iranian Nuclear Issue' (see http://www.armscontrol.org/factsheets/Iran_Nuclear_Proposals) containing summaries of the proposals made by both sides in the period 2003 to 2012.

and we will not tolerate it. We want you to give us an understanding that you will not say anything publicly that will undermine us.'*

Indeed, according to the Iranian negotiator Seyed Hossein Mousavian, the British were completely open with him about this US influence. As we have already pointed out (see page 12), Mr Mousavian claims that John Sawers, head of the British negotiating team, told him explicitly that 'Washington would never tolerate the operation of even one centrifuge in Iran'.

The EU3 eventually made its proposal to Iran for long-term arrangements on 5 August 2005.† This required Iran to make 'a binding commitment not to pursue fuel cycle activities other than the construction and operation of light-water power and research reactors'.‡ In other words, all enrichment and related activities on Iranian soil had to cease for good.

Iran was required to make permanent its voluntary suspension of these activities and to make arrangements for the supply of reactor fuel from abroad, which experience had shown could be cut off at any time.

---

* Seymour Hersh, 'The Iran Plans: Would President Bush Go to War to Stop Tehran from Getting the Bomb?', *The New Yorker*, 17 April 2006

† IAEA Information Circular (see http://www.iaea.org/Publications/Documents/Infcircs/2005/infcirc651.pdf)

‡ Ibid, paragraph 34

In these circumstances, it would be unwise for Iran to contemplate embarking on a significant nuclear power programme for electricity generation.

The UK, France and Germany had broken the commitment they had made at the outset to recognise Iran's right under the NPT to the peaceful use of nuclear energy, subject always to 'objective guarantees'. This change meant, furthermore, that Iran was being invidiously singled out as the only party to the NPT that was forbidden to have uranium enrichment on its own soil.

It was no surprise therefore that Iran rejected these proposals out of hand. And so an historic opportunity was lost for Europe to come to a comprehensive settlement with Iran on a wide range of issues including its nuclear programme.

A missed opportunity

More than once during these negotiations, Iran made proposals to the EU3 offering 'objective guarantees' that its nuclear programme would be peaceful. The offer described in Chapter One, made on 23 March 2005, was the most comprehensive and significant. It included two measures which greatly reduced the possibility that Iran could produce either high-enriched uranium or plutonium, the fissile material for nuclear weapons:

(i) Immediate conversion of all low-enriched uranium to fuel rods for power reactors, to preclude the possibility of further enrichment to high-enriched uranium;

(ii) No reprocessing of spent fuel rods, thereby precluding the production of plutonium.

Iran also proposed the continuous on-site presence of IAEA inspectors at the conversion and enrichment facilities. Nevertheless, the EU3 did not accept the plan as a basis for negotiation, simply leaving it to wither on the vine.

On another occasion, Iran suggested that the IAEA, which was after all the acknowledged specialist in these matters, be asked to suggest appropriate 'objective guarantees'. President Chirac of France agreed that the IAEA was 'in the best position to define such mechanisms' but the proposal was dropped (according to Seyed Hossein Mousavian) because the US was opposed.*

---

* Seyed Hossein Mousavian, *The Iranian Nuclear Crisis*, p164

Finally, in a speech to the United Nations on 17 September 2005, President Ahmadinejad made Iran's most remarkable offer of all. He suggested that Iran's enrichment programme be managed by an international consortium, with Iran agreeing shared ownership with other countries. Once again, this offer was rejected out of hand by the EU and the United States.*

It is reasonable to conclude that the EU states were not interested in devising 'objective guarantees that Iran's nuclear programme is exclusively for peaceful purposes'. Their goal was to halt permanently the core elements of the programme – uranium enrichment and related activities.

Indeed this objective has been explicitly acknowledged by one of the negotiators. Peter Jenkins was the

---

* http://www.globalsecurity.org/wmd/library/news/iran/2005/iran-050918-irna02.htm. Ahmadinejad's suggestion was based on the recommendations of an IAEA expert group, headed by Bruno Pellaud, the former head of IAEA Safeguards. The group was set up to recommend measures that would be useful in giving reassurance that nuclear facilities for civil purposes, for example, facilities for uranium enrichment, which a state has a right to possess under the NPT, would not be used for weapons development. Its report, 'Multilateral Approaches to the Nuclear Fuel Cycle', published in February 2005 (see http://www.iaea.org/NewsCenter/News/2005/fuelcycle.html) contained five proposals, two of which were based on the notion of shared ownership or control. Critics are entitled to point out that Ahmadinejad may not have been in a position to deliver on this proposal.

UK ambassador to the IAEA during this period, and involved in these EU3 negotiations with Iran. Last year he confirmed that Iran offered significant additional safeguards in 2005 and acknowledged:

> With hindsight, that offer should have been snapped up. It wasn't, because our objective was to put a stop to all enrichment in Iran. That has remained the west's aim ever since, despite countless Iranian reminders that they are unwilling to be treated as a second-class party to the NPT – with fewer rights than other signatories – and despite all the evidence that the Iranian character is more inclined to defiance than buckling under pressure.[*]

This remark by Peter Jenkins is unimpeachable evidence that the obstacle to a settlement with Iran in 2005 was the refusal of the EU3 to recognise Iran's right under the NPT to uranium enrichment on its own soil. Iran's flexibility with regard to its nuclear programme, in sharp contrast, is not in doubt.

Sir Richard Dalton and five other former ambassadors

---

[*] Peter Jenkins, 'The Deal the West Could Strike With Iran', *The Daily Telegraph*, 23 January 2012

to Tehran from European countries wrote the following in June 2011:

> We often hear that Iran's refusal to negotiate seriously left our countries no other choice but to drag it in 2006 to the Security Council. Here too, things are not quite that clear. In 2005 Iran was ready to discuss an upper limit for the number of its centrifuges and to maintain its rate of enrichment far below the high levels necessary for weapons. Tehran also expressed its readiness to allow intrusive inspections, even in non-declared sites. But at that time Europe and the US wanted to compel Iran to ditch its enrichment programme entirely. Iranians assume that this is still the European and US goal, and that for this reason the Security Council insists on suspension of all Iranian enrichment activities. But the goal of 'zero centrifuges operating in Iran, permanently or temporarily' is unrealistic, and has contributed greatly to the present stand-off.[*]

---

[*] Sir Richard Dalton, 'Iran is Not in Breach of International Law', *The Guardian*, 9 June 2011. The other ambassadors were Steen Hohwü-Christensen (Sweden),

This letter is further proof that the dogmatism which stood in the way of a settlement in 2005 had its roots in Washington (and London, Paris and Berlin) and not in Tehran.

Iran restarts its nuclear programme

What happened next was inevitable, given the aggressive posture of the United States and Europe. Iran restarted the various nuclear activities it had voluntarily suspended during the negotiations. The resumption began just before Mahmoud Ahmadinejad took over from Mohammed Khatami as Iranian president on 3 August 2005.

As a result, France and Britain persuaded the IAEA Board to pass a resolution on 24 September 2005, which for the first time mentioned the word 'non-compliance' in connection with Iran's nuclear activities. The phrase is of vital importance because the IAEA statute requires any 'non-compliance' to be reported to the Security Council – and this is exactly what happened in March 2006.

Paul von Maltzahn (Germany), Guillaume Metten (Belgium), François Nicoullaud (France) and Roberto Toscano (Italy).

The grounds for this reference to the Security Council were, however, very dubious. To explain why, it is necessary to quote the technical and highly convoluted language of the IAEA resolution. It said: 'Iran's many failures and breaches of its obligations to comply with its NPT Safeguards Agreement, as detailed in GOV/2003/75, constitute non-compliance in the context of Article XII.C of the Agency's Statute.'

GOV/2003/75 is a report by Mohamed ElBaradei to the Board on 10 November 2003 (that is, nearly two years earlier). In other words, the resolution stated that Iran had been in 'non-compliance' in November 2003. However, it also stated that 'the Director General in his report to the Board on 2 September 2005 noted that good progress has been made in Iran's correction of the breaches and in the Agency's ability to confirm certain aspects of Iran's current declarations.'

So, Iran was referred to the Security Council, not because of current 'non-compliance' that needed to be punished, but because of past 'non-compliance', which had largely been corrected.

As Mohamed ElBaradei later acknowledged, the main reason for the referral was so that the Security Council could halt Iran's perfectly legitimate uranium-enrichment programme:

What made Iran's eventual referral a cause for cynicism was that there was nothing new in its 'non-compliance', which had essentially been known about for two years. Recent developments had been positive: the agency had made substantial progress in verifying Iran's nuclear program. The eventual referral, when it came, was primarily an attempt to induce the Security Council to stop Iran's enrichment program, using Chapter VII of the UN Charter to characterise Iran's enrichment – legal under the NPT – as 'a threat to international peace and security'.*

Beginning on 31 July 2006, the Security Council passed six Chapter VII resolutions on Iran's nuclear programme, demanding, inter alia, that Iran suspend its uranium enrichment. Four of these resolutions imposed economic sanctions.

There is every reason to question the validity of these Security Council resolutions, however. Before passing a Chapter VII resolution, the Security Council must decide that a 'threat to the peace' exists† and therefore

---

* Mohamed ElBaradei, *The Age of Deception*, pp146–7

† Or that a 'breach of the peace, or act of aggression' has taken place.

that action is required by the Council to 'maintain or restore international peace and security'.*

But there was no plausible basis for the assertion that Iran's nuclear activity constituted a 'threat to the peace' in 2006. Iran had no nuclear weapons and its nuclear facilities were under IAEA safeguards. And the IAEA hadn't uncovered any attempt to divert nuclear material for possible military use.

Just two months earlier, in May 2006, speaking about Iran's nuclear activities at the Monterey Institute of International Studies, Mohamed ElBaradei said: 'Our assessment is that there is no imminent threat … there is no clear and present danger.'†

We therefore believe that the UN Security Council was acting outside the terms of the UN Charter in passing Chapter VII resolutions imposing economic sanctions on Iran.

---

* UN Charter, Article 39. The action may be to impose economic sanctions on a malefactor under Article 41 of the Charter.

† Quoted in Sammy Salama and Elizabeth Salch, 'Iran's Nuclear Impasse: Give Negotiations A Chance', Center for Nonproliferation Studies at the Monterey Institute of International Studies, 2 June 2006, http://cns.miis.edu/stories/060602.htm

Sanctions imposed

Four of these six resolutions included tranches of economic sanctions. These UN-approved sanctions were limited, because Russia and China opposed more severe ones. They were directed primarily at individuals and entities allegedly involved in the Iranian nuclear and missile programmes. They didn't have much impact on the Iranian economy as a whole and therefore didn't hurt ordinary Iranians.

The US used to make a virtue of this – in January 2010, Secretary of State Hillary Clinton said: 'Our goal is to pressure the Iranian government, particularly the Revolutionary Guard elements, without contributing to the suffering of the ordinary [people], who deserve better than what they currently are receiving.'*

Times have changed. Sanctions imposed by the US beginning in 2012 have done, and continue to do, real damage to the Iranian economy. President Obama boasted of this success during his re-election campaign: in a debate with Mitt Romney on 22 October 2012, he said:

---

* http://www.state.gov/secretary/rm/2010/01/134671.htm

> We … organized the strongest coalition and the strongest sanctions against Iran in history, and it is crippling their economy. Their currency has dropped 80 percent. Their oil production has plunged to the lowest level since they were fighting a war with Iraq 20 years ago. So their economy is in a shambles.*

No worries there about contributing to the suffering of ordinary Iranians.

These are not UN sanctions – they were not prescribed by the Security Council in a resolution under Article 41 of the UN Charter.

They owe their existence to legislation passed by the US Congress in December 2011 at the behest of the pro-Israel lobby in the US. The legislation was accepted by President Obama, who was loath to offend the lobby in the upcoming election year.

The legislation requires the US administration to bully other states around the world to stop (or at least reduce) purchases of Iranian oil, by threatening to cut

---

* www.nytimes.com/interactive/2012/10/23/us/politics/20121023-third-presidential-debate-obama-romney.html. The Iran-Iraq war was, of course, 30 years ago.

off their financial institutions from the US financial system, if they conduct transactions with the Central Bank of Iran or other Iranian financial institutions. Additional sanctions have been imposed since. None of this affects US trade with Iran since it has been negligible since the Islamic Revolution in 1979.

As usual, the EU (including Britain) didn't need to be bullied – they imposed a total ban on oil imports from Iran beginning in July 2012.

At the time of writing, ordinary Iranians are suffering considerable hardship as a result of these sanctions. It is now difficult for Iran to make payments for imports of any kind, because it is cut off from the international banking system. As a result, although pharmaceuticals are not included in the sanctions regime, some life-saving drugs are unobtainable and patients are at risk of death as a result.*

Iran doesn't deserve to be the subject of economic sanctions – it hasn't attacked another country in the

---

* Julian Borger and Saeed Kamali Dehghan, 'Iran Unable to get Life-saving Drugs Due to International Sanctions', *The Guardian*, 13 January 2013: 'Hundreds of thousands of Iranians with serious illnesses have been put at imminent risk by the unintended consequences of international sanctions, which have led to dire shortages of life-saving medicines such as chemotherapy drugs for cancer and bloodclotting agents for haemophiliacs.'

past 200 years, it isn't occupying territory not its own,* it hasn't got any nuclear weapons, it hasn't even got an ongoing nuclear weapons programme, in the view of US intelligence, and therefore by no stretch of the imagination can it be regarded as a 'threat to the peace'.

Britain shares in the responsibility for this appalling state of affairs whereby patients are being deprived of life-saving drugs in Iran. To endanger the lives of innocent civilians in a country that has engaged in aggression, and deserves to be sanctioned, is difficult to justify. To endanger the lives of innocent civilians in Iran today is impossible to justify.

---

* The UAE would disagree: in 1971, after Britain left the Gulf region, Iran took over three small islands in the Gulf, also claimed by the UAE, and has occupied them to this day.

CHAPTER SEVEN

MYTHS, FALSEHOODS AND MISREPRESENTATIONS
ABOUT IRAN

At this point it may be helpful to state the basic facts about Iran's nuclear activities:

+ Iran has no nuclear weapons.
+ Since 2007, US intelligence has held the opinion that Iran hasn't got a programme to develop nuclear weapons and has regularly stated this opinion in public to the US Congress.
+ The IAEA does not assert that Iran has an ongoing nuclear weapons programme.
+ Iran does have uranium-enrichment facilities. But as a party to the NPT, Iran has a right to engage in uranium enrichment for peaceful purposes. Other

parties to the NPT, for example, Argentina and Brazil, do so. Iran is not in breach of any of its obligations under the NPT.

+ As required by the NPT, Iran's enrichment facilities are open to inspection by the IAEA, as are its other nuclear facilities. Over many years, the IAEA has verified that no nuclear material has been diverted from these facilities for possible military purposes. Iran is enriching uranium up to 5% U-235, which is appropriate for fuelling nuclear power reactors for generating electricity, and up to 20% U-235, which is required for fuelling the Tehran Research Reactor.

+ While Iran's nuclear facilities are open to IAEA inspection, those of Israel and India (allies of the United States) are almost entirely closed to the IAEA. Yet Iran, which has no nuclear weapons, is the object of ferocious economic sanctions and threats of military action. By contrast, Israel (with perhaps as many as 400 nuclear bombs, and the capacity to deliver them anywhere in the Middle East) is the object of more than $3 billion a year of US military aid.

These are basic facts about Iran's nuclear activities, facts that are (if you search for them) in the public domain.

Yet the mainstream media in Britain rarely mentions any of them. As a result, almost all of its reporting is misleading, and some of it completely false.

A significant portion of the media just carries on its merry way as if these facts do not exist. It asserts, for example, that Iran already possesses nuclear weapons or has an active programme to develop them.

The BBC, the British state-owned broadcaster, has been guilty of this. On 15 February 2012, its flagship *Ten O'Clock News* began a report on Iran's nuclear activities by stating that 'Iran has announced new developments in its nuclear weapons programme'. This report simply took it for granted that Iran possessed a nuclear weapons programme.

Here is another example. *The Times* carried an article on 20 February 2012, entitled 'Defiant Iran cuts off oil to Britain and France', which reported that 'UN nuclear inspectors [are] due in the country today to gather evidence of Iran's illicit atomic weapons programme'. It went on to refer to 'Tehran's atomic weaponry', giving readers the false impression that Iran's programme had already borne fruit.

As a result, the newspaper's leading article the following day read like propaganda rather than evidence-backed analysis: 'It should be beyond doubt at this stage that Iran is trying to develop a nuclear weapon. Protestations of a desire only for a civilian nuclear capacity have always rung hollow in the fourth-largest oil producer in the world, and lately even Iranian spokesmen seem incapable of delivering them without an accompanying smirk.'

Here is a third example, this time from Sir Max Hastings, the influential journalist and military historian. 'The issue,' wrote Sir Max, 'of whether Iran's march towards ownership of nuclear weapons should be reluctantly accepted or halted by force is one of the most difficult and divisive of our times.'* Sir Max is here accepting without question or examination two propositions for which there is no serious evidence. First, that Iran is hell-bent on the acquisition of nuclear weapons and, second, that the only way to prevent this is through force. Sir Max's cheerful and freewheeling ignorance of the very serious subject he is discussing leads him to airily dismiss the possibility of a peaceful resolution of the Iranian nuclear argument.

In February 2012, *The Economist* referred to 'Iran's nukes' in an article about Hillary Clinton's achievements

---

* Max Hastings, *The Sunday Times*, 4 November 2012. Review of *Mullahs Without Mercy: Human Rights and Nuclear Weapons* by Geoffrey Robertson, and *Nuclear Iran: The Birth of an Atomic State* by David Patrikarakos

as Secretary of State.* The fact that what is normally such a measured, sceptical and authoritative magazine can casually talk of Iran as if it already possessed nuclear weapons highlights the extent to which Iran's presumed guilt is embedded in British and American public discourse.

However, falsehoods such as these are not the only problem with mainstream media accounts. Commentators and others often omit the basic facts and by so doing foster the impression that Iran's nuclear activities are suspect, and that it is difficult to conceive of a purpose for them other than nuclear weapons development.

It then follows that the concerns about these activities expressed by the west, and by Israel, are justified and, if these valid concerns cannot be laid to rest, then ultimately military action to destroy Iran's nuclear facilities, particularly its uranium-enrichment facilities, would also be justified.

---

* *The Economist*, 'Hillary Clinton Bows Out: A Legacy at Foggy Bottom', 9 February 2012, http://www.economist.com/news/united-states/21571478-few-improvements-state-department-legacy-foggy-bottom: 'She may not have brought peace to the Middle East, dealt with Iran's nukes or permanently reset relations with Russia, but Mrs Clinton can be said to have changed the State Department itself for the better.'

In this way, the general media narrative has continually added weight to the proposition that Iran's nuclear ambitions must be curbed, enhancing the case for ever-harsher economic sanctions and, if that fails to do the job, for military action. In this, the mainstream media is behaving as it did in the run-up to the invasion of Iraq in 2003, when, instead of questioning every aspect of the case for military action, it became a cheerleader for war.

Meanwhile, that same mainstream media – so assiduous in presenting the American and Israeli case against Iran – is woefully negligent in presenting the Iranian point of view. As a redress to this, we present in the Appendix Ayatollah Khamenei's eloquent ruminations on nuclear weapons to the conference of the Non-Aligned Movement in Tehran in August 2012.

The mainstream media also persists in presenting Iran as embattled and isolated. This is a parochial view. Iran currently holds the presidency of the Non-Aligned Movement and 120 states were represented at this conference, 24 by presidents, 3 by kings, 8 by prime ministers and 50 by foreign ministers, despite pressure from the US and its allies to discourage attendance. In all, more than 7,000 delegates (and the UN Secretary General) were present. The isolation of Iran is greatly exaggerated.

The Appendix also contains the section dealing with nuclear issues from the Tehran Declaration, which was endorsed by the conference. It emphatically supports the Iranian position.

IAEA Director General's report of November 2011

The mainstream media often suggests that the IAEA Director General's report of November 2011 provides evidence that Iran has an active nuclear weapons programme today. This is not true.

Like all other IAEA reports on Iran, the November 2011 report gives detailed information on the activities at its nuclear facilities. For example, it records the amounts of uranium enriched to 5% and 20% at each facility and confirms that enrichment hadn't taken place to a higher level and that no nuclear material is unaccounted for. This is factual information, based on actual observations by IAEA inspectors on the ground in Iran.

The November 2011 report contains a 15-page annex entitled 'Possible Military Dimensions to Iran's Nuclear Programme'. The 'information' contained in this annex is of a very different character. It consists of allegations – the words 'alleged', 'allegedly' and 'allegation' occur 28 times in total – supplied to the IAEA by third parties, including the US, most of them referring to possible activities by Iran before 2003. US intelligence believes Iran had a weapons programme in this period, which was halted in the autumn of 2003 and hasn't been restarted since.*

Most of the allegations in the annex have been available to the IAEA since 2005 and were already in the public domain. Despite being pressed by the US and its allies to publish them, the previous IAEA Director General, Dr Mohamed ElBaradei, reportedly refused to do so, because they were unsubstantiated allegations that couldn't be verified by the IAEA.†

Dr ElBaradei retired on 30 November 2009. His successor is Yukiya Amano of Japan. The US used its considerable influence to get him elected by the IAEA Board, understandably so, since in the opinion of the US mission to the IAEA, he is 'solidly in the US court on every key strategic decision, from high-level personnel appointments to the handling of Iran's alleged nuclear weapons program' (see WikiLeaks cable dated 16 October 2009).‡

---

* US National Intelligence Estimate, 'Iran: Nuclear Intentions and Capabilities', November 2007

† Flynt Leverett and Hillary Mann Leverett, *Going to Tehran: Why the United States Must Come to Terms With the Islamic Republic of Iran*, p84

‡ http://www.guardian.co.uk/world/us-embassy-cables-documents/230076; see also our extended footnote, p46

It is hardly surprising that, unlike his predecessor, Director General Amano acceded to US demands that the allegations supplied by the US and other third parties be published under the name of the IAEA and thereby be given credibility.

The annex of the November 2011 IAEA report contained little that was new – and did not present evidence that Iran has an active nuclear weapons programme today. In support of this, here are the views of a number of experts on the matter:

Joseph Cirincione, who served on Hillary Clinton's International Security Advisory Board (and is the president of the disarmament group, the Ploughshares Fund): 'I was briefed on most of this stuff several years ago at the IAEA headquarters in Vienna. There's little new in the report. Most of this information is well known to experts who follow the issue.'*

Professor Paul Pillar, who retired from the CIA in 2005 after 28 years' service, his last post being National Intelligence Officer for the Near East and South Asia: 'Despite references in the surge of report commentary about new evidence on this or that aspect of the subject,

---

* Quoted in Seymour Hersh, 'Iran and the IAEA', *The New Yorker*, 18 November 2011

the report told us nothing of importance to policy on Iran that was not already well known.'*

Peter Jenkins, who, as we have noted, was the UK's ambassador to the IAEA from 2001 to 2006: 'The IAEA says that prior to 2003 Iran researched some of the know-how needed for a weapon, and that further research may have taken place in the years since. The IAEA has not reported evidence of attempts to produce nuclear weapons, or of a decision to do so.'†

Dr Hans Blix, former head of the IAEA: 'The IAEA did not … conclude that Iran was making a weapon or had taken a decision to make one.'‡

IAEA Director General Amano was interviewed on the BBC Radio 4 *Today* programme on 17 October 2012. Asked if Iran was 'doing more than simply pursuing a peaceful nuclear programme', he replied: 'We are not saying that Iran has nuclear weapons, nor are we saying that Iran has made a decision to manufacture nuclear weapons.'

So, although the IAEA says that Iran may have engaged in weapons-related activity up to 2003, it does

---

not assert that it has an active weapons programme today. US intelligence agrees and so, it appears, does Israeli intelligence. In April 2012, Benny Gantz, chief of the Israeli Defence Forces, said that he did not believe that Iran would develop nuclear weapons, arguing that Iran 'is going step by step to the place where it will be able to decide whether to manufacture a nuclear bomb. It hasn't yet decided whether to go the extra mile. ... I don't think [Khamenei] will want to go the extra mile.'*

Going the extra mile would involve enriching uranium above 20% towards the 90% or more required for a nuclear weapon. Since Iran's enrichment plants are subject to IAEA safeguards, such a step would be soon visible to IAEA inspectors and crossing this 'red line' would, most likely, cause the US and/or Israel to take military action against Iran – and begin a military confrontation that Iran cannot win. Iran is unlikely to go down that path.

Nuclear weapons a 'grave sin', says Supreme Leader of Iran

Iran's leaders have repeatedly denied that they have any ambitions to develop nuclear weapons. What is more,

---

* Quoted in Shashank Joshi, *The Permanent Crisis: Iran's Nuclear Trajectory*, RUSI, Whitehall Paper 79, p35

the Supreme Leader of Iran, Ayatollah Ali Khamenei, has declared the possession of such weapons a 'grave sin'. He did so in a speech to nuclear scientists on 22 February 2012, saying:

> The Iranian nation has never pursued and will never pursue nuclear weapons. There is no doubt that the decision makers in the countries opposing us know well that Iran is not after nuclear weapons because the Islamic Republic, logically, religiously and theoretically, considers the possession of nuclear weapons a grave sin and believes the proliferation of such weapons is senseless, destructive and dangerous.*

There was nothing new in this statement. In 2005, Ayatollah Khamenei issued a fatwa – a religious edict – saying that 'the production, stockpiling, and use of nuclear weapons are forbidden under Islam and that the Islamic Republic of Iran shall never acquire these

---

* 'Iran Will Never Seek Nuclear Weapons: Leader', Press TV, 22 February 2012, http://www.presstv.ir/detail/228014.html

weapons'* and he has repeated this message many times since then.†

Of course, it is not impossible for Khamenei or a future Supreme Leader to reverse this stance. However, as Flynt and Hillary Mann Leverett point out, this 'would mean having to explain – to Iranians and to the entire Shi'a world – how Iran's strategic circumstances have changed to such an extent that manufacturing nuclear arms was now both necessary and legitimate'. They continue:

> That, of course, is not an absolute constraint on Iranian weaponisation. But it would require, at a minimum, a widely perceived and substantial deterioration in the Islamic Republic's strategic environment – most plausibly effected by an Israeli and/or US attack on Iran. It is far from certain that Tehran would opt for weapons acquisition then. But those urging military action to block the Islamic Republic's nuclear

---

* Iran's Statement at IAEA Emergency Meeting, 10 August 2005, http://www.iaea.org/Publications/Documents/Infcircs/2005/infcirc657.pdf, p121

† Juan Cole, 'Khamenei Takes Control, Forbids Nuclear Bomb', *The Browser*, 4 March 2012

advancement advocate a course that would raise the risk of Iranian weaponisation, not reduce it.*

Ahmadinejad threatened to 'wipe Israel off the map'

Another common fallacy concerning Iran is that President Ahmadinejad has threatened to 'wipe Israel off the map', meaning that were he to obtain nuclear weapons he would seek to use them against Israel. This is a fiction, which arose from a mistranslation from Farsi of a remark Ahmadinejad made in a speech on 26 October 2005 to a conference in Tehran.

As American Professor Juan Cole, among others, has pointed out, the remark was a quote from Ayatollah Khomeini, the father of the Islamic Republic, to the effect that 'this occupation regime over Jerusalem must vanish from the page of time' (*in rezhim-e eshghalgar-i Qods bayad as safheh-e ruzgar mahv shavad*).†

This is not a threat to destroy Israel by military action, but the expression of a hope that the present Israeli regime will collapse, just as the Soviet Union

---

* Flynt Leverett and Hillary Mann Leverett, *Going to Tehran: Why the United States Must Come to Terms With the Islamic Republic of Iran*, p87

† http://www.juancole.com/2009/10/top-things-you-think-you-know-about.html

did. It is not a threat to kill anyone, let alone to commit genocide against Jews living in Israel.

Interviewed on Al Jazeera in 16 April 2012, Dan Meridor, Israeli Deputy Prime Minister and Minister of Intelligence and Atomic Energy, admitted that President Ahmadinejad hadn't actually threatened to wipe Israel off the map.*

Speaking at Columbia University on 24 September 2007, President Ahmadinejad proposed a solution in Palestine based on elections. According to a *Washington Post* translation, he said:

> What we say is that to solve this 60-year problem, we must allow the Palestinian people to decide about its future for itself. ... We must allow Jewish Palestinians, Muslim Palestinians and Christian Palestinians to determine their own fate themselves through a free referendum. Whatever they choose as a nation, everybody should accept and respect. ... This is what we are saying as the Iranian nation.†

---

* http://www.aljazeera.com/programmes/talktojazeera/2012/04/2012413151613293582.html

† http://www.washingtonpost.com/wp-dyn/content/article/2007/09/24/AR2007092401042.html

This appears to be an endorsement of a one-state solution, where the government of Israel/Palestine would be determined by all the people – Jews, Muslims and Christians – living in the area. This proposal may or may not be realistic, but it certainly does not involve 'wiping Israel off the map' in the sense of exterminating Jews and others living there.

It should also be noted that Iran voted for UN General Assembly resolution A/RES/67/19 on 29 November 2012, which backed a two-state solution in Israel/Palestine, specifically, 'an independent, sovereign, democratic, contiguous and viable State of Palestine living side by side in peace and security with Israel on the basis of the pre-1967 borders'. This vote is also not consistent with a determination to 'wipe Israel off the map'.

The general portrayal of Iran as an aggressive state is overblown. By contrast, in the past century, Iran has been the victim of aggression several times – it was invaded and occupied by Britain and Russia during World War I and World War II; it had its democratically elected government overthrown by the US in 1953 at the request of Britain; and it was attacked by Iraq in 1980, with significant subsequent support from the west, and suffered upwards of a million casualties, many as a result of chemical weapons, including around 300,000 killed. The silence of the international community about Iraq's aggression and use of chemical weapons was deafening.

How British politicians spread the nuclear weapons myth

Yet leading British politicians continue to articulate their alarmist talk about Iran's nuclear weapons. In January 2012 British Defence Secretary Philip Hammond spoke of how Iran is believed to be working 'flat out'[*] to build nuclear weapons. The following month British Foreign Secretary William Hague told *The Daily Telegraph* that Iranians were 'clearly continuing their nuclear weapons programme'. This would lead, Hague predicted, 'to the most serious round of nuclear proliferation since nuclear weapons were invented'.[†]

Or listen to David Cameron speaking at the annual dinner of the United Jewish Israel Appeal on 15 October 2012:

> Let's be clear about the facts. Iran is flouting six United Nations resolutions. The regime's

---

[*] Deborah Haynes, 'Iran Working Flat Out on Nuclear Weapons', *The Times*, 6 January 2012

[†] Robert Winnett and Benedict Brogan, 'Iran Risks Nuclear Cold War', *The Daily Telegraph*, 17 February 2012

claim that its nuclear programme is intended purely for civilian purposes is not remotely credible. …

Iran is not just a threat to Israel. It is a threat to the world. Now there are some who say nothing will work – and that we have to learn to live with a nuclear-armed Iran. I say we don't and we shouldn't.

But at the same time I also refuse to give in to those who say that the current policy is fatally flawed, and that we have no choice but military action. A negotiated settlement remains within Iran's grasp. …

We need the courage to give … sanctions time to work. But let me also say this. In the long term, if Iran makes the wrong choice, nothing is off the table. A nuclear-armed Iran is a threat to Israel. And a threat to the world. And this country will work unwaveringly to prevent that from happening.*

Note that the Prime Minister does not explicitly assert that Iran has nuclear weapons or is in the process of

---

* http://www.number10.gov.uk/news/ujia/

developing them. However, he accuses the Iranian leadership of lying when it says that Iran's 'nuclear programme is intended purely for civilian purposes'.

The Prime Minister promised at the outset of his remarks to be 'clear about the facts'. Had he done so he might have made a speech along the following lines:

> Despite the impression given by our media, I don't think Iran's nuclear activities are a threat to the UK. Nobody, not even Israel, believes that Iran has already developed a nuclear weapon. And I would remind you that, since 2007, US intelligence has judged that Iran hasn't even got a programme to develop nuclear weapons. We in the UK are not in the business of second-guessing our closest ally on this matter.
>
> Of course, we all know that Iran has constructed uranium-enrichment facilities. But as a party to the NPT, it has a right to engage in uranium enrichment for peaceful purposes, like other parties to the NPT, for example, Argentina and Brazil. Under the NPT, Iran is obliged to allow these and other nuclear facilities to operate under the

supervision of the IAEA. And it is doing so. In several years of operation, the IAEA has never failed to confirm that no nuclear material has been diverted from these facilities for military purposes.

There are a number of aspects of Iran's nuclear activities which need to be clarified. But there are grounds for hope that, as long as Iran is allowed to enjoy its full rights under the NPT, including its right to enrichment, it will be possible to have arrangements in place that will reassure the international community that its activities are for peaceful purposes.

Unfortunately, the Labour Government missed an opportunity to bring about a settlement in 2005. Then, Iranian negotiators offered to take far-reaching measures to reassure the outside world that its enrichment would not be used for making bombs. However, the Labour Government gave in to the Bush administration's demand that Iran cease enrichment on its own soil – that scuppered an agreement with Iran at that time. We shouldn't make that mistake again.

Another point, which is rarely mentioned but I think is important: the Iranian Supreme Leader Ayatollah Khamenei has issued a fatwa – a religious edict – saying that the production, stockpiling, and use of nuclear weapons are forbidden under Islam and that the Islamic Republic of Iran will never acquire these weapons. I think we should take this pronouncement by the Ayatollah seriously. He is Iran's supreme religious and political leader and the person who would take any decision to develop nuclear weapons. If he intends to do so, it is surely unwise of him to declare repeatedly that these weapons are un-Islamic.

I hope that we can soon terminate the destructive economic sanctions against Iran that are bringing so much misery to ordinary Iranians. After all, the US Secretary of State did promise back in January 2010 to target economic sanctions on 'the Iranian government, particularly the Revolutionary Guard elements, without contributing to the suffering of the ordinary [people], who deserve better than what they currently are receiving'.

Unfortunately, ordinary Iranians are suffering now. We must keep our promises to Iranian people and put a stop to this as soon as possible.

Finally, as a founder member of the UN and a permanent member of the UN Security Council, the United Kingdom is conscious of the obligations of all UN members under Article 2.4 of the UN Charter to refrain from the threat or use of force against other states. It is time for a moratorium on threats of force against Iran, which are in breach of the UN Charter and may even hinder a peaceful diplomatic solution. Let the international community resolve to settle this dispute with Iran by peaceful means, as we should have done in 2005.

CHAPTER EIGHT

SO WHAT IS REALLY GOING ON?

Unfortunately, there seems to be not the faintest chance that Mr Cameron will make a speech of this sort. Instead, the Prime Minister seems intent on doing what the United States tells him, which means applying harsher and harsher economic sanctions, and perhaps taking part in military action, against Iran.

What accounts for the strange and irrational conduct of western leaders? The only explanation is that their antagonism towards Iran may not stem solely from a conviction that Iran is developing nuclear weapons or might do so in future.

Some other motive must be at work. Indeed, President George W Bush made this explicitly clear in his memoir *Decision Points* about his time in office, published in November 2010. The book contains a revealing passage in which the President describes his reaction when the National Intelligence Estimate (NIE) landed on his desk in November 2007. This concluded that Iran hadn't got an active nuclear weapons programme – which was a very awkward conclusion for him, so awkward that it made him 'angry'.*

NIEs are formal assessments on specific national security issues, expressing the consensus view of the 16 US intelligence agencies, which are signed off by the Director of National Intelligence. This one stated: 'We judge with high confidence that in fall 2003, Tehran halted its nuclear weapons program.' It added: 'We assess with moderate confidence Tehran had not restarted its nuclear weapons program as of mid-2007...'.†

One would have expected that the President, who claimed to be dedicated to preventing Iran acquiring nuclear weapons, would have been delighted to receive intelligence that suggested his administration had been successful, that Iran had abandoned an active nuclear weapons programme within three years of his entering the White House.

---

* George W Bush, *Decision Points*, pp418–9 (Kindle Edition)
† US National Intelligence Estimate, 'Iran: Nuclear Intentions and Capabilities', November 2007

But instead he was 'angry'. As the President explained: 'The NIE didn't just undermine diplomacy. It also tied my hands on the military side. There were many reasons I was concerned about undertaking a military strike on Iran, including its uncertain effectiveness and the serious problems it would create for Iraq's fragile young democracy. But after the NIE, how could I possibly explain using the military to destroy the nuclear facilities of a country the intelligence community said had no active nuclear weapons program?'

He concluded: 'I don't know why the NIE was written the way it was. I wondered if the intelligence community was trying so hard to avoid repeating its mistake on Iraq, that it had underestimated the threat from Iran. I certainly hoped that intelligence analysts weren't trying to influence policy. Whatever the explanation, the NIE had a big impact – and not a good one.'

As George W Bush's book acknowledges, US antagonism towards Iran does not stem from a conviction that Iran is developing nuclear weapons or may do so in future. It is about the US determination to prevent Iran becoming a major power in the Middle East in opposition to the US. A change in regime to one that is prepared to do US bidding would be ideal, but that is probably outside the realms of possibility.

For now, the name of the game is to keep the pressure on Iran by ferocious economic sanctions and other means, leaving open the option of military action, justified as a measure to prevent Iran developing nuclear weapons.

To construct and maintain a coalition for this purpose, Iran has been portrayed as a dangerously aggressive state, despite the fact it hasn't started a war in the past 200 years, has no nuclear weapons and has only modest conventional military capacity.

Consider the facts: Iran spends $10–15 billion on arms annually; the US spends $700 billion, about 40% of the total world expenditure on arms.* Iran has no nuclear warheads; the US has upwards of 8,000.† According to a *Washington Post* article in June 2010, at that time the US had special forces deployed in 75 countries,‡ and in August 2011 the Pentagon said that this number was likely to go up to 120, that is,

---

* 'Military Spending: How Much Does the Military Cost Each Country, listed', *The Guardian*, 17 April 2012, http://www.guardian.co.uk/news/datablog/2012/apr/17/military-spending-countries-list

† 'Status of World Nuclear Forces', Federation of American Scientists, http://www.fas.org/programs/ssp/nukes/nuclearweapons/nukestatus.html

‡ Karen DeYoung and Greg Jaffe, 'US "Secret War" Expands Globally as Special Operations Forces Take Larger Role', *The Washington Post*, 4 June 2010

60% of the states in the world.* Iran is believed to have forces in Syria and Lebanon.

Here is a difficult truth. It is the United States, Israel and Britain – and not Iran – who break international law. Hardly a week has passed in recent years without Israel, or the US, or the UK threatening to use military force against Iran. All three are therefore guilty of persistently issuing threats contrary to Article 2.4 of the UN Charter, which requires that all UN member states 'shall refrain in their international relations from the threat or use of force against the territorial integrity or political independence of any state'.

There is little question that all three should be expelled from the UN under Article 6 of the Charter, which provides for the expulsion of a member that 'has persistently violated the Principles contained in the present Charter'. That's not going to happen, of course, since two of the miscreants are veto-wielding members of the Security Council (which must recommend any expulsion) and the other is their close ally.

That's the way the UN system works, or rather doesn't.

---

* Nick Turse, 'A Secret War in 120 Countries', *The American Conservative*, 4 August 2011, http://www.theamericanconservative.com/articles/a-secret-war-in-120-countries/

And consider this: thanks to the hypocrisy and double standards of the west, Iran would be within its rights to withdraw from the NPT and remove the constraints upon it due to Treaty membership. Article X says:

> Each Party shall in exercising its national sovereignty have the right to withdraw from the Treaty if it decides that extraordinary events, related to the subject matter of this Treaty, have jeopardized the supreme interests of its country. It shall give notice of such withdrawal to all other Parties to the Treaty and to the United Nations Security Council three months in advance. Such notice shall include a statement of the extraordinary events it regards as having jeopardized its supreme interests.

By any objective standard, Iran and other neighbours of Israel have good grounds for withdrawal, because of the build-up over the past 40 years of an Israeli nuclear arsenal directed at them. There could hardly be a better example of 'extraordinary events, related to the subject matter of this Treaty', which 'have jeopardized [their] supreme interests'. It might not be wise for Iran to with-draw from the NPT at the present time, since it would risk terrible havoc from the US/UK and/or Israel. But, there is no doubt that such an action would be fully justified under the provisions of the NPT.

CHAPTER NINE

A PLEA FOR SANITY

For more than 30 years, predictions have been made by the west and Israel that Iran is on the verge of acquiring nuclear weapons.* Time and time again these predictions have proved to be inaccurate.

In 1984, *Jane's Defence Weekly* reported that Iran's production of a bomb is 'entering its final stages'. This 'information' allegedly came from West German intelligence sources.

In 1992, the current Israeli Prime Minister Benjamin Netanyahu claimed that Iran was three to five years

---

* Scott Peterson, 'Imminent Iran nuclear threat? A timeline of warnings since 1979', *Christian Science Monitor*, http://www.csmonitor.com/World/Middle-East/2011/1108/Imminent-Iran-nuclear-threat-A-timeline-of-warnings-since-1979/Earliest-warnings-1979-84. The subsequent quotations from *Jane's Defence Weekly*, President Netanyahu and the *New York Times* (p96) are all from Peterson.

from being able to produce a nuclear weapon – and that the threat had to be 'uprooted by an international front headed by the US'.

In 1995, *The New York Times* reported that senior US and Israeli officials feared that 'Iran is much closer to producing nuclear weapons than previously thought' – about five years away.

In 2007, President Bush warned that a nuclear-armed Iran could lead to 'World War III'.* A month later, however, a US National Intelligence Estimate (NIE) expressed the opinion with 'high confidence' that Iran had halted its nuclear weapons programme in 2003.[†]

No dispassionate observer can fail to note the dangerous similarities between the aggressive talk which surrounds today's nuclear stand-off and the confrontation with Mossadeq 60 years ago. Sixty years ago there was the same blinkered refusal by the west to countenance reasonable demands.

Mossadeq, like the Iranian leadership today, was portrayed as a pantomime villain – and compared to Hitler by both *The Wall Street Journal* and *The New*

---

* Press Conference, 17 October 2007, http://georgewbush-whitehouse.archives. gov/news/releases/2007/10/20071017.html

† US NIE, 'Iran: Nuclear Intentions and Capabilities', November 2007

York Times. The London *Observer* (a liberal newspaper) damned Mossadeq as a 'fanatic' and a 'tragic Frankenstein' who was 'obsessed with one xenophobic idea.'*

No American newspaper presented Iran's grievances in a fair-minded way. In 1964, Richard Cottam, who worked as a US diplomat in Iran in the 1950s, wrote that press coverage of the Mossadeq period bordered on the 'grotesque, and until that era is seen in truer perspective there can be little hope for a sophisticated US foreign policy concerning Iran.'† Sadly, nothing has changed in the intervening 60 years. The country is portrayed with the same caricatures, the same baffled incomprehension, the same ossified ignorance; and the same deep-seated cultural and political arrogance are at work.

We are not asserting that Iran is a perfect western liberal democracy, and we acknowledge that the regime has been guilty of human rights abuses that no humane

---

* Quoted in Pankaj Mishra, 'Why Weren't They Grateful?', *London Review of Books*, 21 June 2012

† Ibid, pp 19–20. We have drawn our comparison with the Mossadeq era heavily from Mishra's article, a review of Christopher de Bellaigue's *Patriot of Persia*, cited above. Mishra adds: 'In *The US Press and Iran: Foreign Policy and the Journalism of Deference* (1988) William Dorman and Mansour Farhang show that no major American newspaper had ever spelled out Iran's grievances against the AIOC (Anglo-Iranian Oil Company). Rather, *The Washington Post* claimed that the people of Iran were not capable of being "grateful".'

and detached observer can ignore. Yet Iran's western critics rarely for their part accept that Iran is a complex and sophisticated civilisation, where female university students outnumber men, and where the state is far less repressive than Saudi Arabia, a close ally of the United States and the west. It is also important to note that the militant 'Islamist' threat to the west (whether from the attack on the Twin Towers in New York on 9/11, the 7/7 bombings in London or similar threats) comes from an extremist Sunni ideology that has its roots in Saudi Arabia and emphatically not from Shi'a Islam.

Nor are we pretending for one moment that Iran has been faultless in its dealings with the rest of the world over its nuclear ambitions. Iran certainly breached its safeguards agreement with the IAEA in the 1990s. The IAEA believes that there were military dimensions to its nuclear programme, prior to 2003 and maybe since. More recently, Iran breached its safeguards agreement by failing to inform the IAEA of its decision to build a second enrichment plant near Qom at the time the decision was made (though the plant has been operating under IAEA safeguards since). It is perfectly reasonable for the rest of the world to view Iran with a degree of distrust in the light of the secrecy over Qom and other episodes.

However, Iran's transgressions are not a reason to hound it forever. Indeed, such a course of action would be spectacularly counterproductive. South Korea and Egypt, for example, have also breached their safeguards obligations, but not been punished at all. As we have seen, Israel and India have actually been rewarded after they secretly developed the nuclear bomb. Iran currently has every reason to be suspicious of an international community which seems determined to single it out for unfair treatment.

Not everyone in the British and American foreign policy establishment is blindly ignorant. In a most encouraging interview with the *Financial Times* in June 2009,* Senator John Kerry, then Chairman of the Senate Foreign Relations Committee, described the inflexibility on Iran by the Bush administration as 'bombastic diplomacy' that 'wasted energy' and 'hardened the lines'. Under the NPT, Iran had 'a right to peaceful nuclear power and to enrichment in that purpose,' he said. If these views of John Kerry in 2009 were to become the US policy propounded by Secretary of State Kerry in 2013, the prospects for a settlement with Iran on the nuclear issue would be excellent.

---

* Daniel Dombey, *Financial Times*, 'US Senator Opens Iran Nuclear Debate', 10 June 2009

But if not, the outlook for the world is grim. The sanctions regime being imposed on Iran is not only unjust. It's dangerous. It is the way that wars start.

It's time we asked some difficult questions about ourselves, and why we in the west have felt such a need to stigmatise and punish Iran. We need to face the fact that Iran is an independent nation with legitimate interests. Once we do that, and accept that Iran has every right to enrich uranium for peaceful purposes, under close safeguards, we may find it surprisingly easy to strike a deal which can satisfy all sides.

APPENDIX

The 16th summit of the Non-Aligned Movement took place in Tehran from 26 to 31 August 2012. At this summit, Iran took over the presidency of the 120-member movement from Egypt. President Mohamed Morsi of Egypt attended and handed over the presidency to President Ahmadinejad.

As we pointed out in Chapter Seven, 120 states were represented at the summit, 24 by presidents, 3 by kings, 8 by prime ministers and 50 by foreign ministers, despite pressure from the US and its allies to discourage attendance. In all, more than 7,000 delegates (and the UN Secretary General) were present.

The following is the section of Ayatollah Khamenei's inaugural address to the summit on 30 August 2012 dealing with nuclear issues:*

> Honorable audience, international peace
> and security are among the critical issues of
> today's world and the elimination of cata-
> strophic weapons of mass destruction is an
> urgent necessity and a universal demand.
> In today's world, security is a shared need
> where there is no room for discrimination.
> Those who stockpile their anti-human weap-
> ons in their arsenals do not have the right
> to declare themselves as standard-bearers of
> global security. Undoubtedly, this will not
> bring about security for themselves either.
> It is most unfortunate to see that countries
> possessing the largest nuclear arsenals have
> no serious and genuine intention of remov-
> ing these deadly weapons from their military
> doctrines and they still consider such weap-
> ons as an instrument that dispels threats and
> as an important standard that defines their
> political and international position. This

---

* http://english.khamenei.ir//index.php?option=com_content&task=
view&id=1668

conception needs to be completely rejected and condemned.

Nuclear weapons neither ensure security, nor do they consolidate political power, rather they are a threat to both security and political power. The events that took place in the 1990s showed that the possession of such weapons could not even safeguard a regime like the former Soviet Union. And today we see certain countries which are exposed to waves of deadly insecurity despite possessing atomic bombs.

The Islamic Republic of Iran considers the use of nuclear, chemical and similar weapons as a great and unforgivable sin. We proposed the idea of 'Middle East free of nuclear weapons' and we are committed to it. This does not mean forgoing our right to peaceful use of nuclear power and production of nuclear fuel. On the basis of international laws, peaceful use of nuclear energy is a right of every country. All should be able to employ this wholesome source of energy for various vital uses for the benefit of their country and people, without having to depend on others for exercising this right. Some western countries, themselves possessing nuclear weapons and guilty of this illegal action, want to monopolise the production of nuclear fuel. Surreptitious moves are under way to consolidate a permanent monopoly over production and sale of nuclear fuel in centers carrying an international label but in fact within the control of a few western countries.

A bitter irony of our era is that the US government, which possesses the largest and deadliest stockpiles of nuclear arms and other weapons of mass destruction and the only country guilty of its use, is today eager to carry the banner of opposition to nuclear proliferation. The US and its western allies have armed the usurper Zionist regime with nuclear weapons and created a major threat for this sensitive region. Yet the same deceitful group does not tolerate the peaceful use of nuclear energy by independent countries, and even opposes, with all its strength, the production of nuclear fuel for radiopharmaceuticals and other peaceful and humane purposes. Their pretext is fear of production of nuclear weapons. In the case of the Islamic Republic of Iran, they themselves know that they are lying, but lies are sanctioned by the kind of politics that is completely devoid of the slightest trace of spirituality. One who makes nuclear threats in the 21st century and does not feel ashamed, will he feel ashamed of lying?

I stress that the Islamic Republic has never been after nuclear weapons and that it will never give up the right of its people to use nuclear energy for peaceful purposes. Our motto is: 'Nuclear energy for all and nuclear weapons for none.' We will insist on each of these two precepts, and we know that breaking the monopoly of certain western countries on production of nuclear energy in the framework of the Non-Proliferation Treaty is in the interest of all independent countries, including the members of the Non-Aligned Movement.

The summit endorsed the Tehran Declaration.* The following three paragraphs are taken from the section

---

* http://www.nam.gov.ir/Portal/File/ShowFile.aspx?ID=6d1ea997-6620-465d-881c-e4f64970415b

in the declaration dealing with nuclear issues. They emphatically support the Iranian position:

> 5. Nuclear weapons are the most inhumane weapons ever conceived. The maintenance of strategic and tactical nuclear stockpile and their continued modernization, as well as new military doctrines setting the rationale for their possible use, particularly against non-nuclear weapon states (NNWS), represent the greatest threat to humankind. The Non-Proliferation Treaty (NPT) did not provide a right for nuclear weapon states to keep their nuclear arsenals indefinitely. States Parties to the NPT have obligations under Article VI of the NPT to destroy all nuclear weapons within a time-bound framework, which is yet to be fulfilled. It is imperative to conclude a comprehensive convention on nuclear disarmament.

> 6. All states should be able to enjoy the basic and inalienable right to the development, research, production and use of atomic energy for peaceful purposes, without any

discrimination and in conformity with their respective international legal obligations. Therefore, nothing should be interpreted in a way to inhibit or restrict the right of states to develop nuclear energy for peaceful purposes. States' choices and decisions, in the field of peaceful uses of nuclear technology and their fuel cycle policies, including those of the Islamic Republic of Iran, must be respected.

7. The inviolability of peaceful nuclear activities should be upheld and any attack or threat of attack against peaceful nuclear facilities operational or under construction amounts to a serious danger to human beings and the environment, and constitutes a grave violation of international law, of the principles and purposes of the Charter of the United Nations, and of regulations of the IAEA. There is a pressing need for a comprehensive multilaterally negotiated legal instrument prohibiting attacks, or threat of attacks on nuclear facilities devoted to peaceful uses of nuclear energy.

INDEX